lines that wiggle

by **candace whitman**

illustrations by **steve wilson**

blue apple books

Text copyright © 2009, 2024
by Candace Whitman
Illustrations copyright © 2009, 2024
by Steve Wilson
All rights reserved
CIP Data is available.
First published in the
United States 2009 by
🍎 Blue Apple Books
South Orange, New Jersey
www.blueapplebooks.com

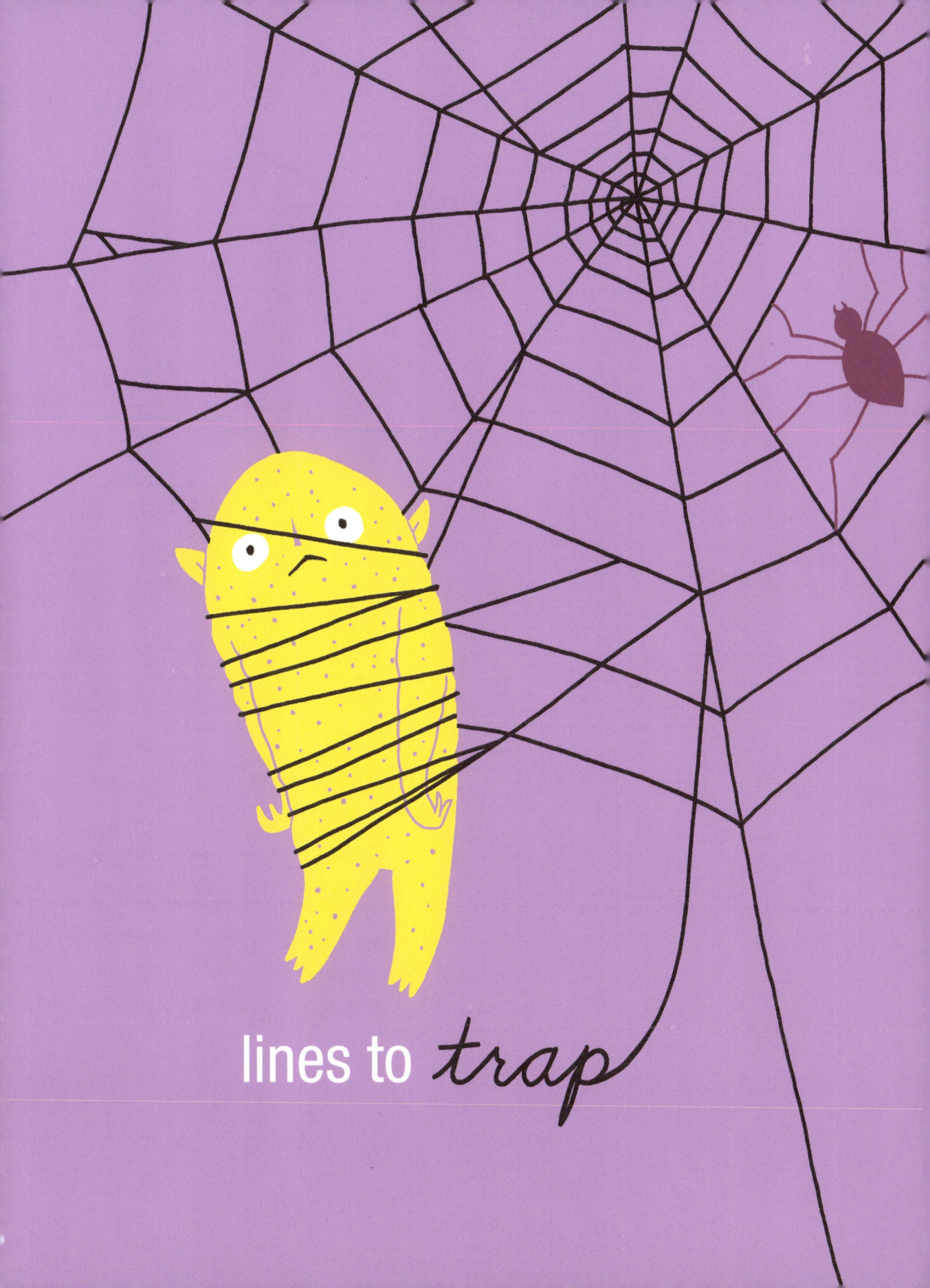

lines that *twist*

lines that *sway*

lines that *swish* the flies away.

www.ingramcontent.com/pod-product-compliance
Lightning Source LLC
Chambersburg PA
CBHW040714290825
31824CB00010B/11